The Letter To Philemon

R. H. Boll

Compiled and Reprinted from
The Word and Work

THE LETTER TO PHILEMON

R. H. B.

As in a dewdrop the whole sun and sky can be mirrored, so a comparatively trifling private affair can become the mirror in which the whole glory and beauty of Christianity is reflected. That is demonstrated in the short letter of Paul to Philemon.

Philemon is not an epistle of *public* scope or importance. It is written by a man to a man about a man. The writer was an inspired apostle, Paul; the man addressed was his friend and brother in Christ, Philemon; and the one concerning whom the epistle treats is Onesimus, a runaway slave of Philemon's. But as unimportant as its whole matter may appear in the view of the wide world's interests, the circumstances set forth in this letter were of deepest concern to the three persons involved. The truths also and principles that shine out through this little inspired writing are of highest importance to us who read it today.

The facts underlying Paul's letter to Philemon are these: Onesimus, a slave, has run away from his master, Philemon, a Christian, and a man of some wealth. Moreover, it is implied that the fugitive slave had also been a thief. The slave Onesimus arrives in Rome, and there, either by chance, or by seeking, finds Paul, who at the time was a prisoner. Through contact with Paul he is converted. Now, first of all, old wrongs must be righted. The severe and unflinching rectitude of the gospel must be vindicated. Onesimus must return to his master.

No one who knows anything about slavery in the days of Rome will underestimate the gravity of the situation. To be a *fugitivus* was an enormous offense, punishable in the most terrible way. A slave had at the best *no rights:* no redress for injuries, no protection against the cruelest injustice, no chance even, however innocent, to answer and vindicate himself against any charge of accusation. Instances enough have come down to us to show how common a thing it was for a slave to have to suffer cruel mistreatment, even unto death by crucifixion, for the merest semblance of a cause, or for no cause at all, save the will of the master or the whim of his mistress. But to be a *fugitive* was a terrible crime, sure of swift and awful retribution. When long-standing custom, backed by law, demands a certain course, it is exceedingly difficult for the individual to forsake the rut, or even to disengage his mind from the power of the current judgment. What would Philemon do in the matter? Public opinion would demand the extremest punishment of the runaway slave. If he should have him beaten unto blood and unconsciousness, it would be all too lenient. There was a hope that the punishment would be mitigated, but what Philemon might do was a sore problem. In the face of all risks, however, *Onesimus must go back to his master.* Such is the high and stern righteousness of the gospel.

It was a great test for the converted slave, a test of the sincerity of his repentance, a test of his courage and of his trust. It was an equally great test to Philemon. Would the gospel prove its power in his case? Would faith and love prevail over long-sanctioned custom and legalized unmercifulness? Between the two, to make each one's test less severe, to draw Philemon to the ways of Christ and to comfort and strengthen Onesimus, intervenes Paul's fervent love in the Lord for them both. And this love expressed itself in the tender and powerful intercession to Philemon for the poor slave redeemed by Jesus' blood. That is the soul and purpose of the epistle to Philemon.

There is tact in this letter: great carefulness and wisdom, a sanctified diplomacy which is not the same as policy and worldly shrewdness; but which springs of the tender regard and consideration and sympathy of a genuine love. As he never at any other time had used flattery, or acted with a double motive (2 Cor. 1:12; 1 Thess. 1:3-5), so all the courtesy and rhetorical skill displayed in this letter were but the sincere and unstudied expression of a heart made tender and sensitive and wise in that true love, which is the fruit of the Spirit. We note first the warmth of the whole-hearted

SALUTATION.

"Paul, a prisoner of Christ Jesus, and Timothy our brother, to Philemon our beloved and fellow-worker, and to Apphia our sister, and to Archippus our fellow-soldier, and to the church in thy house: Grace to you and peace from God our Father and the Lord Jesus Christ."--Verses 1-3.

It is *Paul* that here speaks. What weight and force the beloved name carries to Philemon's heart! But more is to be added--he is now Paul, *the prisoner of Christ Jesus;* that is to say, for Christ's sake he is now in prison; and as he was the Lord's when he was free, so now bound he is the Lord's prisoner. Will thy heart feel the unspoken appeal of this word, O Philemon? *Timothy the brother* joins in the greeting. Now the address: to *Philemon*--and two things he calls him: "*the beloved and fellow-worker.*" Beloved by whom? By the apostle? Surely. But more: by the Lord himself. Not by man, not by the greatest and best of men only, but like Daniel (Dan. 10:11), like the saints at Rome (Rom. 1:8), this brother is the object of Christ's love. May he abide in it! (John 15:9.) And fellow-worker! When we consider the world-wide, age-lasting importance of Paul's great work, what claim had the simple and limited work of a private brother to be mentioned alongside of Paul's? Philemon a fellow-worker of Paul? From God's viewpoint, yes, for He gave to every member in the Body his place and his gift, and made each honorable according to his faithfulness. But there is a sweet condescension in this recognition of Philemon as an apostle's fellow-worker. This also is of love.

Apphia, Philemon's wife doubtless, comes in for special mention. She is "*the sister,*" "*our sister,*" and *Archippus* a son, or a preacher, abiding with them (Col. 4:17), is "*our fellow-soldier.*" Appreciation, though not definitely expressed, stands out in the very form of the salutation. It develops also that *the church* met *in Philemon's house.* It was a common thing in those days for the church to meet in a private home (Rom. 16:5; 1 Cor. 16:19; Col. 4:15), and it would be a good and desirable arrangement now in many more cases than is generally thought expedient.

Now, the apostolic greeting and blessing, *"Grace to you and peace"*--grace before peace, for there can be no peace except through God's free grace. What better thing could be embodied in the blessing than these two? And not favor (grace) from a human source, nor the sort of "peace" that men find in forgetfulness, or in some fool's paradise of New Thought, or the misnamed heresy of "Christian Science," which ignores the real evil and mentally drugs them into a false dream of peace which must sooner or later find a rude awakening--nay, but this peace is *"from God our Father and the Lord Jesus Christ."* It is from Him who met the evil and the curse by his love, the God who alone can give true peace; and from Him who made peace and bought peace at the price of his blood; even the true peace, "the peace of God which passeth understanding." May that grace and peace be ours also!

EXPRESSED WITH THANKSGIVING AND PRAYER

Verses 4 to 7

"I thank my God always, making mention of thee in my prayers, hearing of thy love, and of the faith which thou hast toward the Lord Jesus, and toward all the saints; that the fellowship of thy faith may become effectual, in the knowledge of every good thing which is in you, unto Christ. For I had much joy and comfort in thy love, because the hearts of the saints have been refreshed through thee, brother."

To Paul every true and faithful Christian appeared as a gift of God, good and precious. And truly such they are. Whatever there is of true faith, of love unfeigned, of real goodness, it did not spring out of the fleshly nature of the brethren. Such things come only of the grace of God. If God had left these brethren as natural men, to pursue their own course, and to work out the way of their own nature, they would have been only "children of wrath," even as the rest (Eph. 2:3). If now they are different from "the rest," it is because they are God's workmanship, created over again in Christ Jesus (Eph. 2:10). For their very willingness to do right, and their very efforts to overcome (which is their side of it)--for whatever they have done and accomplished, the praise and the honor belong to God; for it is He that worked in them both to will and to work for His good pleasure

(Phil. 2:13); and they are the trees of God's planting, the work of His hands, that He may be glorified (Isa. 60:2). By the grace of God they are what they are. Well may Paul give God thanks for them--not only on their behalf, but *for them* (1 Thess. 1:2), for they are the living blessings, walking treasures, God's good gift to his own church and to all the world.

"*I thank my God always,*" Paul writes therefore, "*making mention of thee in my prayers.*" For Paul had heard of Philemon's love and faith--likely heard it from this very Onesimus himself--*a love* and *faith* which went out in its fruit both *toward the Lord Jesus Christ and toward all the saints.* His prayer now is for Philemon's future walk--that he might continue, grow, go onward from glory to glory, and from strength to strength. Unlike ourselves, Paul prayed as fervently for the strong Christians as for the weak. Both were urgently in need of God's mercy and help; the one that he may be brought back to the right ways of the Lord; the other that he may not faint nor grow weary, but go on abounding more and more." For it has been well said that "We may never go back, but there is a point from which we will

never go onward." And that, too, means fail-
ure, the more insidious because it often leaves
the heart unaware and self-complacent. When
therefore Paul heard how the gospel had taken
good hold in a church or in a Christian, and was
bearing good fruit, straightway he turned to
intercession on their behalf, that they might
not let up, but press on to better things still
(Eph. 1:15-19; 3:14-19).

So he prays for Philemon "*that the fellowship of thy faith*"--the partnership with the Lord
Jesus Christ, and in the Lord's work, into which
we have entered by faith (1 John 1:3-7)--"*may
become effectual in the knowledge of every
good thing which is in you, unto Christ.*" For
there are great things implanted in us (comp.
Jas. 1:21), gifts which wait to be stirred up
(comp. 1 Tim. 4:14, 15; 2 Tim. 1:6), hidden
blessings and possibilities which await discov-
ery and development--in fact all the virtues and
powers which are comprised in the expression,
"Christ in you the hope of glory" (Col. 1:27),
which came in and became ours when He came
in to make His abode with us. It is not what we
have that does us good, but what we *know* we
have. Let every Christian seek for light and un-

derstanding from God, that he may come into fuller knowledge and possession of "the unsearchable riches of Christ" (Eph. 1:17-19). Then will the fellowship of our faith become *effectual unto Christ.* For he shall be able to bear His fruit in and through us.

And, indeed, Philemon was well on the way. Already he had been drinking of the water Jesus gives (John 4:13, 14); [4] and already it had become in him a well of water springing up unto eternal life; and others had been refreshed from this springing well within him. "*For I had much joy and comfort in thy love, because the hearts of the saints have been refreshed through thee, brother.*" What a refreshing it is when our souls are much discouraged because of the way, to meet with a heart strong and joyful in its faith and love; how it revives us to drink of the sweet streams that flow out of that heart; how our eyes are lightened; how the dark doubts fly, how hope comes and with it renewed courage and confidence! How welcome these well-springs of healing in our time of need, even as when

> " *   * Travelers in a desert land,
> Beneath a burning sky,
> Long for the cooling spring at hand,
> For they must drink or die."

THE INTERCESSION FOR THE SLAVE

Verses 8 to 20

"Wherefore, though I have all boldness in Christ to enjoin thee that which is befitting, yet for love's sake I rather beseech, being such a one as Paul the aged, and now a prisoner also of Christ Jesus: I beseech thee for my child, whom I have begotten in my bonds, Onesimus, who once was unprofitable to thee, but now is profitable to thee and to me; whom I have sent back to thee in his own person, that is, my very heart: whom I would fain have kept with me, that in thy behalf he might minister unto me in my bonds of the gospel: but without thy mind I would do nothing; that thy goodness should not be as of necessity, but of free will. For perhaps he was therefore parted **from thee** for a season, that thou shouldest have him forever; no longer as a servant, but more than a servant, a brother beloved, specially to me, but how much rather to thee, both in the flesh and in the Lord. If then thou countest me a partner, receive him as myself. But if he hath wronged thee at all, or oweth **thee** aught, put that to mine account; I Paul write it with mine own hand, I will repay it: that I say not unto thee that thou owest to me even thine own self beside. Yea, brother, let me have joy of thee in the Lord: refresh my heart in Christ."

At last Paul comes to his point. He has carefully prepared the way for it. A man will lend an ear to those who think well of him and love him. Paul's love and appreciation for Philemon were the best assurance that Philemon would listen to Paul's request. And then, it is not amiss for a brother to be reminded of his past goodness and good work in Christ. We all have a strong inclination for consistency, whether in evil or good. If we have begun to do wrong, it is easy enough to look back and make our present conduct of a piece with our former. A similar pull lies in our past good deeds, to draw us yet onward unto more of the same sort of thing. Philemon's past faithfulness and love will stand him in good stead now in this present test (for a great test it is). The precedents he set for himself in former days, and the habit and character of Christlikeness he had thus far wrought out, will help him to do the Christ like thing now. For what I do today helps or hinders me in tomorrow's trial, according to whether it is good or bad.

The apostle could have commanded. As the ambassador of the Lord he had the right and the authority to do so. It is good that Philemon should remember this, and that, after all, Paul's words are not so much Paul's as the Lord's. If the act required had been one that involved less of the tender emotions than this present act of mercy which Paul was about to demand of Philemon, and which, if it is to be worth anything, must not be strained--Paul might have commanded. In fact if the appeal of love failed, he might have commanded. But it is not an outward performance done perfunctorily, if not sullenly, that was wanted; but a deed of tender love. Love must ask here, and Love must draw forth love; so that Philemon might not act "grudgingly or of necessity," but that he might do it freely, under the constraint of the love of Christ. For when a man acts in love he is free.

The law of love frees us from all other commandments. *"Wherefore, though I have all boldness in Christ to enjoin thee that which is befitting, yet for love's sake I rather beseech."* This throws a light on some other of Paul's beseechings (1 Cor. 1:10; 2 Cor. 5:20; Rom. 12:1). It was the beloved Paul beseeching--*"Paul the aged,"* grown old in the service of Christ; nay, now even in prison in the Lord's bonds. Paul counts on Philemon's love; Philemon will not say to him nay. But behind Paul it is Christ beseeching, yea, God himself--"as though God were entreating by us" (2 Cor. 5:20). Did Philemon understand that? Thus does our love for Christ work through our love for his servant. It is not independent of Christ's servants, for it is through them that He becomes known and is loved. For that cause Paul strove to magnify Him in his body, whether by life or by death. Who loves the Lord Jesus Christ because he has known and loved you, my brother? Yet the time may also come when we must love Him independently, when all men shall fail us, and we must look to Him alone. That will be a still greater test.

Finally comes the name of the unfaithful, unworthy slave--a name which at the beginning of the letter might have roused up an indignation, which, however just, might easily have shut the door to reason and entreaty. But Paul was thoughtful of Philemon. "I *beseech thee for my child Onesimus.*" "*Paul's child?*" muses Philemon as he reads--"Of whom can he be speaking? Surely not the fugitive slave." But yes-- even he, "*Whom I have sent back to thee in his own person, that is, my very heart.*" Now all wrath must stop, and all thought of vengeance and retribution becomes impossible. To touch Onesimus is to strike the heart of Paul--it will never do. If Paul loves him so, then I must treat him as Paul himself. For so does the knowledge of the love of God work in us. First of all I begin to realize how very dear I [6] am to Him. (1 John 4:10.) Next it grows upon me that my brother is as dear to Him as I am. I must love him for God's sake. Philemon was well caught. The meshes of the love net Paul had thrown over them were closing in and binding him on every side. Yet the skillful fisher of men continued to draw. "*Who once was unprofitable to thee,*" truly he had been a worthless wretch-- "*but now*"--O believe in the transforming power of Christ through the gospel! "*but now is profitable to thee and to me.*"

"*Whom I would fain have kept with me, that in thy behalf he might minister unto me in the bonds of the gospel.*" As Philemon reads his wonder grows and with it confidence and affection toward the new and different Onesimus springs up. "Not on my account only," Paul would say, "do I ask you to receive Onesimus with love and regard: he himself is a different man: worthless once, worthy now; once of no account, now so able and helpful that I should like to have kept him to help me in my gospel-work!" The only reason why Paul sends him is that he would not presume upon Philemon's goodness by forcing a good work upon him. For if it were not wholly of Philemon's will and own choice to give Onesimus to Paul for a helper, it would count nothing for Philemon. God accepts no such forced benevolence. Love respected the rights of Philemon in the matter, and looked on his interests, and guarded his privilege of personal choice. It is too common for Christians to force and push one another into good works. But Paul says, "*Without thy mind I would do nothing, that thy goodness should not be as of necessity but of free will.*"

But back to Onesimus. Paul discerns God's special providence in this case. The inspired apostle expresses here the knowledge and conviction that God does such things. Although in no wise implicated in the wrong of which Onesimus was guilty, God had so overruled and used the circumstance to give him back to his master, a redeemed man, that Philemon might have him in a higher possession forever. "*For perhaps he was therefore parted from thee for a season, that thou shouldest have him forever; no longer as a servant, but more than a serv-ant, a brother beloved, specially to me, but how much rather to thee, both in the flesh and in the Lord.*"

It would seem at this point that Paul had said enough and had pleaded in full for Onesi-mus. But not yet. The apostle sweeps the ground thoroughly, and leaves not a splinter that might hinder the path of the desired rec-onciliation. "If Onesimus has stolen anything"--nay, it is too hard a word--"*if he hath wronged thee at all,*" or if his escape has put you to fi-nancial loss, and thus "*he oweth thee aught, put that to mine account; I Paul write it with mine own hand, I will repay it: that I say not un-*

to thee that thou owest to me thine own self besides." So Paul would himself make good any financial deficit if Philemon were disposed to make a difficulty of that--which of course he would not; in fact, he could not since Paul stood security, not that thereby the deficit was covered, but because it would be out of question to let Paul pay it, seeing Philemon owed Paul his very life. So the bad account of Onesimus must needs be cancelled if not for Onesimus' sake, at least for the love of Paul who assumes all Onesimus' liabilities.

Thus does Paul take the part of the poor runaway slave, and even identifies himself with him. It cannot be summed up in better words than these of Martin Luther:

"This epistle showeth a right noble, lovely example of Christian love. Here we see how St. Paul layeth himself out for the poor Onesimus, and with all his means pleaded his cause with his master; and so setteth himself as if he were Onesimus, and had himself done wrong to Philemon. Yet all this doeth he not with power or force, as if he had right thereto; but he stripped himself of his right, and thus enforceth Philemon to forego his right also. *Even as Christ did for us with God the Father, so doth Paul for Onesimus with Philemon:* for Christ also stripped Himself of His right, and by love and humility enforced[*] the Father to lay aside His wrath and power, and to take us to His grace for the sake of Christ, who lovingly pleadeth our cause, and with all His heart layeth Himself out for us. *For we are all His Onesimi,* to my thinking."

Which, with a bit of reasonable allowance for the figure, is very true indeed.

CONCLUSION AND SALUTATIONS

Verses 21 to 25

"Having confidence in thine obedience I write unto thee, knowing that thou wilt do even beyond what I say; but withal prepare me also a lodging: for I hope through your prayers I shall be granted unto you. "Epaphras, my fellow-prisoner in Christ Jesus, saluteth thee; and so do Mark, Aristarchus, Demas, Luke, my fellow-workers.   "The grace of our Lord Jesus Christ be with your spirit. Amen."

There is a reassurance in these last words. "I did not plead because I doubted you, Philemon, or thought it needful to persuade you with argument. I know your readiness to follow God's will in every matter, and while I am writing I am assured that you will not only do all I ask, but more," says Paul in effect. As the delicate seismograph senses the slightest tremor of the earth's crust from afar, so Paul's sensitive heart feels that Philemon might be grieved. "Did Paul think it necessary to write to *me* on this fashion? Did he think he needs to plead so insistently in order to persuade an unwilling heart to do that which is good and noble in God's eyes?" "Nay brother," replies Paul, "I *knew* you were willing and full of love. The mention of the right course, the suggestion of my wish and God's will, are enough. You will do, and more than do, all that I ask."

A final personal message: "*Prepare me also a lodging.*" I am coming. How does Paul know? Possibly the prospects were that he would be released from the Roman prison in the near future. But Paul ever recognizes the hand of God in his life; and the fact that *God's movements are affected by the prayers of His children.*

There was in Paul none of that dead rational-ism which repudiates whatever it cannot un-derstand--which, so far as it can, explains the supernatural out of the universe, or the Bible, or the Christian faith; and in respect to the lat-ter dares to say that prayer has no effect save by reflex action upon the person that prays. Paul said, and strictly meant, "*I hope that through your prayers I shall be granted unto you again.*" My unbelieving friend may ask here, "How could the prayers of a few Chris-tians in Asia affect the course of Roman justice and open the gates of the imperial prison to a prisoner?" But the answer to that question is not difficult to the believer. God's word has it so. If the prayers of the Lord's disciples could affect the movements of an army so that a cer-tain siege would not occur at a season unfavor-able to flight (Matt. 24:20)--or numbers of simi-lar examples--we may confidently believe that God hears prayers and can act in response to them. The "how" is his; ours it is to believe and to pray.

Epaphras, also in prison in the Lord (for wherever a Christian is and whatever he does is "in Christ"), and others who were near Paul,

Mark (probably the same Mark whom Paul had once refused to take with him, Acts 15:36-40) *Aristarchus, Demas* (who later forsook Paul, preferring the present world, 2 Tim. 4:10) *Luke,* "the beloved physician," and writer of Acts and of the gospel that bears his name--send salutation to Philemon.

And as he set out with the benediction of grace and peace, so now he closes with a like doxology:

"The grace of our Lord Jesus Christ be with your spirit. Amen."

* Luther's word "enforce" might leave the impression that Christ by His work persuaded (or even compelled) God to spare the sinner. Christ's work was indeed necessary to our salvation; but God Himself was the Author of it all. It was **He** that gave His Only Beloved--**He** sent Him and delivered Him up for us all. It was by the Father's will that Christ gave Himself for our sins. God did not need to be persuaded, but by the Father's arrangement the sinless Son of God came and bore our sins that God might be just and the justifier of him that believeth on Jesus. (Rom. 3:25, 26.)

Made in the USA
Coppell, TX
12 July 2024